Bibliographic information published by the German National Library:

The German National Library lists this publication in the National Bibliography; detailed bibliographic data are available on the Internet at http://dnb.dnb.de .

Imprint:

Copyright © 2015 GRIN Verlag, Open Publishing GmbH
Print and binding: Books on Demand GmbH, Norderstedt Germany
ISBN: 978-3-668-08003-4

This book at GRIN:

http://www.grin.com/en/e-book/309614/a-framework-for-managing-the-security-risks-to-customers-on-the-mobile

Ireneus Mathias

A framework for managing the security risks to customers on the mobile payment ecosystem in Tanzania

GRIN Publishing

GRIN - Your knowledge has value

Since its foundation in 1998, GRIN has specialized in publishing academic texts by students, college teachers and other academics as e-book and printed book. The website www.grin.com is an ideal platform for presenting term papers, final papers, scientific essays, dissertations and specialist books.

Visit us on the internet:

http://www.grin.com/

http://www.facebook.com/grincom

http://www.twitter.com/grin_com

A FRAMEWORK FOR MANAGING THE SECURITY RISKS TO CUSTOMERS ON THE MOBILE PAYMENT ECOSYSTEM IN TANZANIA

Ireneus Rugashoborora Mathias

Masters of Science in Information Technology and Management (MSc. IT & M) Thesis
Avinashilingam University (INDIA)

July, 2015

A FRAMEWORK FOR MANAGING THE SECURITY RISKS TO CUSTOMERS ON THE MOBILE PAYMENT ECOSYSTEM IN TANZANIA

By

Ireneus Rugashoborora Mathias

A Thesis Submitted for Fulfillmentof the Requirements forthe Degree of Masters of Science
in Information Technology and Management (MSc. IT & M) of the

Avinashilingam University (INDIA)

Avinashilingam University (INDIA)

July 2015

ACKNOWLEDGEMENT

This thesis would never have seen the light of the day without the ideas, support, and assistance of numerous people. In the following lines, I would like to take the opportunity to express my gratitude to the persons that supported me most.

First and foremost, my deepest thanks is to all my lectures for the course of Master of Science in Information Technology and Management for 2013 – 2015 from the Avinashilingam University (INDIA) and Institute of Finance Management (TANZANIA) who contributed their valuable advice and guidance during the course of this project work so that I increased my knowledge.

It is a pleasure to thank my supervisor Dr. Rose Tinabo, the Head of Information Technology at the Institute of Finance Management (IFM), for her scientific guidance, constant support and the valuable feedback regarding diverse aspects of my research until I managed to complete my report.

I extend my sincere thanks to Mr. D. Koloseni and Mr S. Mutama, the MSc ITM Coordinators, for their tireless assistance, guidance and encouragement; and Dr. Jamal Adam, the Lecturer for Research Methodology and Statistical Techniques, for his invaluable specialist input into this study. Without their support this project would have been an uphill task.

I also convey my sincere gratitude to all my fellow students and friends for their assistance in my study. I am grateful to all respondents of the study questionnaire for their cooperation as without their inputs, this thesis would not have been completed.

Last, but most of all, I want to thank my parents for teaching me to become what I am. Likewise, I express my sincere gratitude to my wife Anastasia Protas and my daughters, Irene - Peace Byera and Ingrid - Peace Shubi for their love, encouragement, and trust throughout my study period.

Thank you all!

JULY 2015   IRENEUS RUGASHOBORORA MATHIAS

DEDICATION

I dedicate this thesis work to all customers vulnerable to security threats on the mobile payments in Tanzania.

ABSTRACT

The trend of mobile payment businesses in Tanzania is steadily growing with the potential to revolutionize cash dominant economy to cashless which remarks the growing of financial inclusion in the country. However, that development brings many issues regarding customer security in Tanzania due to insufficient knowledge of users, poor information delivery channels, lack of appropriate legal infrastructure and inappropriate security properties.

This study intended to propose a framework for addressing the potential security risks to customers on the mobile payments in Tanzania. In fulfilling that objective, the study explored the potential security risks to customers; the roles of the mobile payments stakeholders in securing customers; the legal gaps in customer security; the liability for securing customers and lastly proposed a framework for managing the security risks to customers on the mobile payment.

The research was a case study of the potential security risks to customers on the mobile payments in Tanzania and used exploratory and descriptive approaches to enable familiarization of the potential security risks to customers on the mobile payments in Tanzania and better data analysis. The study employed purposive sampling techniqueto draw a sample and used a structured questionnaire tocollect data. Data were captured by using SPSS and analyzed with MS Excel. Both qualitative and quantitative research approaches were used for better interpretation and presentation of findings.

By synthesizing the literature review and empirical findings, this thesis has proposed a framework for managing security risks to customers on mobile payments in Tanzania. The core elements of this framework include collaboration of stakeholders, risk management program, customer awareness program and legal and policy reforms. This study recommends legal and policy reforms to accommodate mobile payment customer security issues.

TABLE OF CONTENTS

LIST OF FIGURES

LIST OF TABLES

ABBREVIATIONS AND ACRONYMS

AML/CFT	-	Anti-Money Laundering and Combating the Financing of Terrorism
APPs	-	Alternative payment providers
BOT	-	The Bank of Tanzania
GSM	-	Global System for Mobile communications
GSMA	-	Groupe Speciale Mobile Association
ICT	-	Information and Communication Technology
ISACA	-	Information Systems Audit and Control Association
ISO	-	International Organization for Standardization
ITU	-	International Telecommunication Union
KYC	-	Know Your Customer.
MFS	-	Tthe mobile financial services
MNO	-	Mobile network operators
MPSP	-	Mobile payment service provider
MTN	-	Mobile Telephone Networks Holdings
OECD	-	Organization for Economic Co-operation and Development
P2B	-	Person to Person
P2P	-	Person to Business
PSD	-	Payment Services Directive
SMS	-	Short Message Service
STK	-	SIM Application Toolkit
TCRA	-	The Tanzania Communications Regulatory Authority
USAID	-	United State Agency for International Development
USSD	-	Unstructured Supplementary Service Data
WAP	-	Wireless application protocol

CHAPTER ONE: INTRODUCTION

1.1   Introduction

This chapter provides background to the study, a statement of the problem, research objectives, and the scope of the study. It also presents limitations of the study and the research structure.

1.2   Background of the study

The mobile network operators (MNOs) in Tanzania have emerged to be new payment institutions, providing cash in and cash out services, remittance, airtime top-up, bill payments, and loan repayment through the mobile phones. Such payments through the mobile phones are called mobile payments (USAID, 2013; ITU, 2013).Mobile payments haveimproved the efficiency of financial services and lowering transaction costs of which have inspired greater consumers' confidence, and high usage (OECD, 2012).

The rapid public acceptance of mobile payment services in many countries, including Brazil, India, Uganda and Kenya has demonstrated real benefits to people who previously could not access financial services (ITU, 2013). In Tanzania, Osikena, 2012 argues thata tremendous usage of mobile phones to deliver financial services is catalyzed by the increasing convergence of service providers, financial institutions and communication sector.

The growth of the mobile payments in Tanzania is quantified by the Bank of Tanzania (BOT) statistics for 2013 and the GSMA report for 2014, that there are more than 11 million subscribers for four mobile payment platforms, offering mobile money services. These are Vodacom (M-PESA) which was launched in 2009, Tigo (TigoPesa) and Zantel (Z-Pesa) launched in 2010 and Airtel (Airtel Money) launched in 2011.

However, the growth of mobile payments give rise to a number of security threats to users, such as privacy violations, malware attacks, fraud, theft, deviations in the quality of services, financial and device losses (Komba, 2013). These threats are attributed by ignorance, technical issues, lack of effective regulations, inadequate information about the mobile transactions and lack of proper complaints and redress mechanisms (Ally, 2012; Inter Media, 2013).

So far, these security threats to users have received little attention in Tanzania. Unfortunately, the existing laws do not suffice to address the risks associated with the Mobile Financial Services (MFS) such as loss, fraud, and privacy concerns to customers. Yet, the available studies on mobile payments in Tanzania provide no solutions to such vulnerabilities (ITU, 2013).

To tackle such threats, Pegueros (2012) and Gadja (2011) propose customer educationto enhance users' responsivenesswhile, the Consumers International (2012) and theEuropean Payments Council (2014) proposes access to information, right to consumer safety, right to consumer redress; and promotion of economic interests of consumers. These mechanisms have their origins in the Universal Declaration of Human Rights.

Other mechanisms to secure customers in the mobile payments are effective laws, collaboration of the involving parties, use of passcode and automatic lock out, mobile malware protection, enhanced mobile payment infrastructure and automatic software updates (Scribbins, 2013).

Basing on various models for managing security risks to customers, this study has proposed a framework containing four major core elements, including the collaboration of stakeholders, risk management program, customer awareness program and legal and policy reforms. The proposed framework to secure customers on the mobile payments needs to be reviewed and modified regularly to keep pace with the dynamic technological advancement and market forces.

2

1.3 Statement of the problem

The explosive growth of mobile payment services in Tanzania demonstrates the potential transition of unbanked and poor communities into mainstream financial inclusion (Ally, 2012). Such growth of mobile payments in Tanzania has brought substantial benefits to many people like facilitating payments (Komba, 2012) and personal saving (InterMedia, 2013).

However,on the other hand the development of mobile payment system has given rise to enormous security implications to customers in Tanzania, particularly privacy violation, incidents of theft, fraud, device and financial losses; malware attacks, insufficient information about the terms and conditions of a transaction, and the absence of redress system to resolve disputes between merchants and consumers (OECD, 2012; ITU, 2013).

Despite the aforementioned security risks on the mobile payment ecosystem, yet there is no empirical survey so far which provides solutions to control those potential risks facing customers in the mobile payment ecosystem in Tanzania (Ally, 2012; Komba, 2013). The absence of feasible mechanism to control the potential risks associated with the development of mobile payments expose more than 11 million mobile money subscribers in Tanzania into vulnerabilities (GMSA, 2014).

This scenario called for the need for a comprehensive study with the intent of proposing the solution to address the customers' multiple vulnerabilities on the mobile payment ecosystem so as to promote financial inclusion in Tanzania.

1.4   Research Objectives

The general objective of this study is to propose a framework that would address the security threats to customers on the mobile payment ecosystem in Tanzania. Furthermore, this thesis presents the following objectives:-

a) To identify the potential security risks to customers on the mobile payment ecosystem.

b) To identify the roles of stakeholders in securing customers in the mobile payments.

c) To examine the laws related to customer security on the mobile payments in Tanzania.

d) To examine the liability of securing customers on the mobile payments in Tanzania.

e) To develop the framework for addressing the security risks to customers on the mobile payment value chain ecosystem in Tanzania.

1.5   Research Questions

The central research question of this study was: What is an appropriate framework for addressing the potential security threats to customers on the mobile payment value chainecosystem in Tanzania? This central research question results in the following sub questions, namely:-

a) What are the potential security risks to customers on the mobile paymentecosystem?

b) What are the roles of the stakeholders in securing customersin the mobile payments?

c) What are the laws related to customer security on the mobile payments in Tanzania?

d) Who is liable for securing customers on the mobile payments ecosystemin Tanzania?

e) Which framework can be put in place to address security risks to customers on the mobile payment value chain in Tanzania?

1.6   Scope of the Study

The aim of this study was topropose a framework that would address the security threats to customers on the mobile payment ecosystem in Tanzania. All research objectives were set to achieve this target. Thus, this study concentrates on that subject matter and examined how better obligations the mobile payment players can fulfill to secure customers. All other details apart from the subject matter of this project are not discussed.

1.7   Motivation

A need to secure customers on the mobile payment ecosystem arises due to the rapid growth of Information and Communication Technologies (ICT) and the convergence of MNOs and other service providers in the mobile payment value chain in Tanzania which are attracting many customers including those unbanked while accompanied by increasing security risks to customers who are already sidelined by the traditional banking.

Yet the present practical measures to countercheck mobile payment risks on the end users are insufficient as pointed out by Harris et al. (2013). This gap is stressed by ITU (2013) that the mobile payment market in Tanzania only provides a strong supervisory framework to electronic money issuers to protect them against operational and financial risks rather than securing mobile payment end users with strong laws, policies and technical assistance.

This thesis presents a framework which focuses on the solution for the potential security risks to customers on the mobile payment in Tanzania.The framework integrates the roles of the mobile payment stakeholders, customer education programs, laws and legal reforms with respect to customer security on the mobile payments so as to create a secure environment for mobile payment diffusion as a catalyst for financial inclusion to the mass.

1.8 Limitation of the study

The study involved a considerable number of mobile payment customers, the TCRA, MNOs and bank officials and other stakeholders emerging from ICT, legal and security background. This research did neither include non-registered users of the mobile payment services.

According to the GSMA, (2014) the mobile payment active users in Tanzania are more than 11 million, of which are not heavenly distributed in the country. Therefore, it should be noted that the research findings of this study are limited to only one district in Tanzania.

From the questionnaire, there was a response rate of 96% and the non-response rate of 4%. The high response rate could be due to the reason that, 250 questionnaires were sent to the mobile payment outlets where the agents were asked to distribute them to their customers coming in for mobile payment transactions and ensure that these questionnaires were duly filled and returned.

The questionnaires were administered by the MNO mobile money agents. As a result the personal relationship with the agents administering the survey could also indirectly influence the respondents to provide feedback they deem right and not what actually happens in practice. To overcome these limitations, the researcher worked within the time frame and scope of the study.

1.9 Research Structure

This thesis starts with the Chapter 1. This chapter presents the background of the study, problem statement and the research objectives. It also provides the reader with research objectives, the scope of the study, research motivation and the organization of the thesis (structure). Chapter 2 review literatures related to the subject matter. Chapter 3 presents the research methods and Chapter 4 discusses research findings. The proposed framework to address security risks to customers on the mobile payment ecosystem in Tanzania is presented and discussed in Chapter 5. This thesis ends with the summary, recommendations and conclusion in Chapter 6.

CHAPTER TWO: LITERATURE REVIEW

2.1   Introduction

This chapter discusses the revolution of mobile payments and the mobile payment arena in Tanzania. It also discusses the mobile payments business models, the security of mobile payments, the potential security threats facing customers on the mobile payment and the strategies to mitigate security risks facing customers on the mobile payment system.

2.2   Mobile payments revolution in Tanzania

The Federal Reserve (2013) defines a mobile payment as purchases, payments to another person, or any other payments made using a mobile phone. The ITU (2013) describes mobile payment or m-payment as any payment where a mobile device is used to initiate, authorize and confirm an exchange of financial value in return for goods and services over a mobile telecommunication network which can be made independent from the payer's location. Mobile devices in this case include mobile phones, tablets or any other devices that are able to connect to mobile telecommunication networks and enable payment to be made (UNCTAD, 2012).

Access to finance is a key challenge for populations in the developing countries, where many are unbanked and financially excluded due to low income levels and a general lack of brick and mortar infrastructure that meant that traditional banking models are not economical to deploy. As a result, the revolution of the mobile payment solutions as alternative payment providers (APPs) bridges the gap and enables the unbanked and underbanked mobile phone users to access financial services. Moreover, the adoption of mobile payments is on an upward curve in Tanzania attracting more than 11 million active customers (UNCTAD, 2012; USAID, 2013; GSMA, 2014).

The mobile money landscape in Tanzania is currently dominated by four mobile money platforms, namely Vodacom (M-PESA), Tigo (Tigo-Pesa), Zantel (Z-Pesa) and Airtel (Airtel Money) deploying a total of more than 153,369 agents, with more than 31.8 million subscribers, of which 11 million are active customers. The Tanzania's mobile payment market share is dominated by Vodacom's M-Pesa with 53%, followed by Tigo-Pesa with 18% and Airtel Money with 13% (GSMA, 2014).

In 2007 the Mobipawa platform was introduced in Tanzania by E-fulusi Africa Limited. The Mobipawa mobile payment solution allowed its subscribers to transfer, receive, and withdraw money as well as purchase goods and services by using mobile phones (Msamila, 2014).

In 2008 the Bank of Tanzania (BOT) issued letters of no objection to Vodacom (T) Ltd and Zantel allowing them to carry out mobile payment businesses (Di Castri 2014). Vodacom Tanzania launched M-Pesa in April 2008 and on the same year Zantel entered the mobile payment market with its product branded as Ezy-Pesa extending from its Zanzibar market base to the mainland Tanzania (Di Castri, 2014). M-Pesa and Ezy-Pesa enabled their customers to send and receive money and effect payments by using mobile phones (Masamila, 2014).

In 2009, Airtel (T) Ltd, formerly known as Zain introduced Airtel Money, a mobile payment platform developed by Hamisco Oberthur technologies. Airtel through AirtelMoney has interlinked with several banks of which enabled its customers to manage their virtual money between their Airtel Money and bank accounts (Di Castri, 2014).

Thereafter, in September, 2010 Tigo introduced mobile payment version called Tigo Pesa that enabled its customer to send and receive money known as personal-to-personal payment (P2P) payment of services (P2B) such as bill and utilities (Di Castri, 2014).

2.3   Mobile payment ecosystem

Mobile payment system encompasses a network of various players forming a business ecosystem which include MNOs that provide mobile infrastructure and customer base using communication services; services providers accepting mobile payments; agent network facilitating cash in-cash out services, regulators of telecommunications and financial institutions that enable the exchange of money between parties; the mobile money users normally subscribed to an MNO's financial services, as well as technology, processes and systems that link and facilitate the delivery of payments systems to mobile money users (UNCTAD, 2012). The mobile payment business ecosystem is a consumer centric system as mobile payment users consume various services provided by different suppliers in the ecosystem (The European Payment Council, 2012).

The recent growth of mobile payments market is pulling in a number of stakeholders in an ecosystem as well as more customers. In turn, this expansion poses pressure on the banking industry, merchants and service providers to invest heavily in more mobile payments products to increase their market share (Daily Nation May 16, 2014; Millicom, 2014). The mobile payment providers deploy competitive advantage parameters such as differentiation, cost effectiveness, innovation, growth, and alliances in offering mobile payment services to their customers (Ernest & Young, 2014).

Such mobile payments business growth enables the mobile payment subscribers in Tanzania to send or receive money, withdraw or deposit cash from mobile agents, withdraw or deposit cash into their respective bank accounts, make payments at retail supermarket chains, cable television, paying for water and electricity bills as well as paying for fuel at selected fuel stations. The players and their roles, interdependences and services offered to customers on the mobile payment ecosystem are hereafter discussed and illustrated in figure 2.1.

9

2.3.1 The mobile network operators (MNOs)

The MNOs play leadership roles within a mobile money ecosystem, responsible for securely routing messages, issuing mobile phone numbers, operating the mobile infrastructure and providing the customer base (ITU, 2013). Today, MNOs are increasingly diversifying their mobile services, through partnerships with banks and various service providers which bring the unbanked and underbanked populations into the organized financial services and assist in furthering the electronic payments market (InterMedia, 2012).

2.3.2 Financial institutions

Financial institutions use the banking infrastructure to enable the exchange of money and regulatory compliance with national financial regulations and policy between different parties involved in the mobile money ecosystem (InterMedia, 2012). Financial institutions provide centers for payments and strong customer relationships in the mobile payment ecosystem (ADB, 2012).

In Tanzania financial institutions strategically shape their businesses by entering partnerships with MNOs, MPSPs, merchants and other authorities to implement mobile payment solutions so as to reach unbanked in remote areas and thus promoting quality of service delivery (Jenkins, 2013). For example, banks such as CRDB, NMB and TPB and other financial institutions, in collaboration with MNOs, have embarked on the provision of SMS banking services which allows their customers to use their mobile phones to access their bank accounts, transfer money and make various payments of goods and services (InterMedia, 2013). The new mobile banking services in Tanzania include, Postal Bank's "TPB Popote" and CRDB's "Fahari Huduma" which use agents as banking branches to allow more mobile payment users to formalize their financial activities hence encouraging financial inclusion (Masamila, 2014).

10

2.3.3   Mobile Payment Service Providers (MPSPs)

Mobile Payment Service Providers (MPSPs) are the businesses affiliated to the mobile payment network that are benefiting from the mobile money solution that allow them to make more efficient payment for products and services, direct sales, and micro-credits (InterMedia, 2012). With the mobile payment system, a customer needs to make deposits or payment to the agent and then send or make electronic payments through mobile phones (UNCTAD, 2012). In Tanzania, examples of the MPSPs include MAXCOM and Selcom mobile.

2.3.4   The agent network

The success of the mobile payment system is dependent on a reliable network of agents (UNCTA; 2012). The role of the agent network includesfacilitation of cash-in and cash-out and handle customer services such as registration, account opening, transactions recording and reporting suspicious transactions in accordance with anti-money laundering and countering the financing of terrorism (AML/CFT) and facilitate customer validation (ITU, 2013; USAID 2013).

In East Africa Community (EAC), agent networks have contributed to the success of mobile payment services to reach out the mass (UNCTAD, 2012). However, some of the challenges facing agents include the running out of cash or e-money float (liquidity risks); especially when customers withdraw more than they deposit and vice versa, inappropriate customercare, insufficient trainings and the absence of documentation proof (Intermedia, 2012; USAID, 2013).

Moreover, the USAID report for 2013 recommends that the mobile payment risks and the KYC, AML, and CFT challenges at the agent level can be counteracted through regular business trainings, shared agent networks, interoperability and multiple cash out and float channels like ATMs and Cards so as to improve agent's competence, and capture customers' demand sufficiently (ITU, 2013).

2.3.5 Mobile device manufacturers

The other key component of the ecosystem is the mobile handset makers, chip manufacturers as well as application providers (UNCTAD, 2012). The handset manufacturers such as Nokia, Motorola, Samsung and Apple are gaining a significant market share on the mobile payment ecosystem (Pegueros, 2012). These brands are the best dominants, in Tanzania mobile markets.

2.3.6 Merchants

In the mobile payment ecosystem, merchants accept mobile payments in exchange for different products and services. They help to increase demand for mobile money by offering more avenues through which users can spend their mobile money (UNCTAD, 2012).

2.3.7 Customers of the mobile payment services

Mobile money customers are those users normally subscribed to an MNO's financial services (UNCTAD, 2012). With mobile payment services, customers benefit from reduced risk of carrying cash, increased access and affordability of payment (InterMedia, 2012). As explained by the GSMA (2014) Tanzania has more than 31.8 million people subscribed to mobile payment services, of which 11 million are active customers. These figures of subscriptions outnumber the growth of commercial bank accounts in Tanzania (USAID, 2013).

2.3.8 Regulators

The mobile payments regulatory institutions in Tanzania include the Bank of Tanzania (BoT) for the financial issues and Tanzania Telecommunications Regulatory Authority (TCRA) that regulates issues pertaining to communications infrastructure (Masamila, 2014). Moreover, mobile payments regulators are expected to promote financial inclusion and foster interoperability among payment services and reduce risks of money laundering (ITU, 2013).

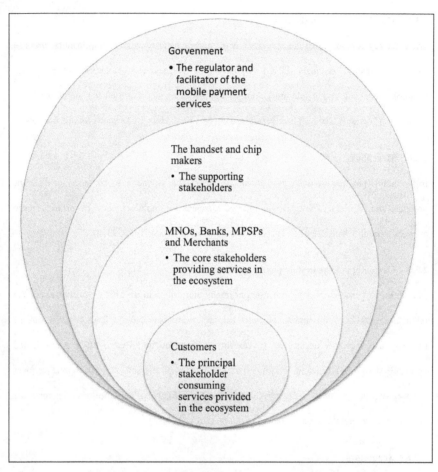

Figure 2.1:   The mobile payment ecosystem (Source: European Payment Council, White Paper on Mobile Payment, 2012)

2.4   Laws related to customer security in the mobile payments in Tanzania

Regulation is essential to maintaining an enabling environment for business, and mobile money is no exception (UNCTAD, 2012). The first concern of the regulation of telecommunications and financial sector is to maintain public confidence in financial services and markets (Ally, 2012). In the EAC, the central banks regulate the financial sector, while telecommunication authorities regulate the communications sector (UNCTAD, 2012).

In Tanzania, some of the pertinent financial laws and legislations that influence the operations of mobile money includethe BOT Act of 2006 which created the BOT; the Banking and Financial Institutions Act of 2006 which provides the legal framework for undertaking banking operations in Tanzania; the Anti-Money Laundering Act of 2006 which helps to address AML/CFT issues and the Tanzania Communications Regulatory Authority Act of 2003 which regulates communications. Others include the Fair Competition Act of 2003 which fosters competition in different sectors and the Electronic and Postal Communications (EPOC), Act 2010 (Parliamentary Acts of Tanzania).

Unfortunately, the above cited laws were either developed before the explosions of mobile financial services or other existing laws do not accommodate issues pertaining to financial transactions through mobile phones. Insufficiency regulations of mobile payment services in Tanzaniaopen a window for all possible anomalies in the system such as money laundering, terrorism financing and vulnerabilities to more than 11 million customers of the mobile payments (Ally, 2012; Di Castri, 2014).

While Tanzania is lagging behind in regulating mobile payments, some developing countries such as Kenya, Mali, Senegal and South Africa, have passed specific laws on mobile payments, and among other concerns, is to address issues on customer security (ITU, 2013).

14

2.5 Security of the Mobile Payment Services

Security of the mobile payment is the major factor in its diffusion and market breakthrough in the world (Federal Reserve, 2013). The purpose of mobile payment security is to enable communications and transactions to take place in a secure environment without fear of compromise, while at the same time disabling non-legitimate activities such as eavesdropping or spoofing, or tampering with data (ITU, 2014).

The mobile payments are enabled by a variety of technologies such as Unstructured Supplementary Service Data (USSD), Short Message Service (SMS), SIM Application Toolkit (STK) and Wireless Application Protocol (WAP). These technologies are needed to address various wireless payment industry needs, including secure authentication on mobile devices, secure transmission and accessibility of virtual money stored on a mobile device (ITU, 2014).

However, these mobile money technologies are not usually secure. For example, SMSapplication used by the Global GCash in Philippines; STK network service used by Mpesa, in Afghanistan, Kenya, South Africa and Tanzania and MTN Mobile Moneyin Africa and USSD used by Airtel Money and Vodacom Mpesa, in Afghanistan, Kenya, South Africa and Tanzania, WIZZT in South Africa, EKO in India, MTN Mobile Money in Africa T Cash in Haiti and Easy paisa in Pakistan involve encryption during transmission between the base transceiver station and the mobile station and the end to end encryption is currently not available of which create vulnerabilities to customer security (ITU, 2013).

However, WAP application can provide better security, as data are encrypted between the customer and the merchant/bank. WAP implementations are more common with banks adding mobile as another channel for users to access their accounts (ITU, 2013).

Moreover, many studies on information security focus mainly on technical and implementation related issues. However, consumers only perceive security from the subjective realm, which is usually incubated through advertisements and public information (Uchena et al. 2008). Security and trust are among the key considerations for adoption of mobile payment systems and thus, the user security needs to be properly addressed (UNCTAD, 2012).

The concept of security has two dimensions, objective and subjective security. While the former is a platform or application security based on concrete technical characteristics, the latter, is the consumer's perceived sensation of the security procedures and it includes confidentiality, integrity, authentication, authorization, availability and non-repudiation (Uchena et al. 2008).

The UNCTAD (2012) insists that any payment systems, must meet the transaction security properties, namely confidentiality, that each engaging party to authenticate the party whom she is communicating with; ensure privacy, that messages are revealed only to the intended recipient; ensure transaction integrity, that the received messages are not altered during transmission; ensure non-repudiation of transactions that no party can deny the transactions she has performed; ensure availability, that users can access services using mobile devices whenever needed and ensure confidentiality, that transmitted and stored data cannot be read by unauthorized parties.

Adopting a security approach that addresses both dimensions of security; objective security with technical characteristics, and subjective security, mostly procedural and from the customer point of view, it is imperative for organizations to take full advantage of business opportunities whilst building customer confidence in the security of their multiple mobile paymentservices they are offering (Uchena et al. 2008). Therefore, the mobile money transfer security approach should not impinge mobile payments adoption so as to promote financial inclusion.

16

2.6 The potential security risks to customers on the mobile payments

The Federal Reserve (2013) identifies that security perception is the major challenge for the adoption of mobile payment services. This implies that, the customers' decision to use mobile money is influenced by threats and risks on the ecosystem. Whitman et al (2012) and ITU (2013) explained threats and risk to include all susceptibilities which endanger users and a probability or threat of damage, injury and any other negative occurrence, respectively.

Pegueros (2012) discusses that the infancy of the mobile payment technology brings many risks in the areas of new technologies due to new, inexperienced entrants, little attention to security as a discipline and a complex supply chain with risks in the secure integration of the complex ecosystem. Pegueros (2012) and Harris et al. (2013) contend that ignorance of the most customers over the mobile payment technologies is the main cause of their privacy vulnerability.

Loss of mobile devices, theft, fraud, unauthorized access, financial losses, privacy violations, malicious applications, SMS vulnerabilities, hardware and operating system vulnerabilities, liquidity, delayed transactions, money laundering and lack of complaint system are some of the identified mobile payment risks to customers. For example, the smallsize of mobile phones not only make customers vulnerable to misplacement, theft, losses and fraud, but also is a security threat to people with cognitive, physical, or sight problems (Pegueros, 2012; Harris et al., 2013).

A liquidity risk is a major challenge to customers wishing to deposit or withdraw money due to lack of cash or electronic float at an agent outlet, particularly in the EAC as pointed out in the UNCTAD report for 2012. Likewise, regular system downtime, delayed transaction by a network and deviations of quality of services due to unreliable power also increase the risks of carrying cash to customers (Inter Media, 2013; ITU, 2013).

17

Current mobile device versions are designed to acquire, install, and use third-party applications. This poses security risks to users, especially for mobile device platforms that do not place security restrictions or other limitations on third party applications. Downloading free software may increase the risk of mobile malware infections that an attacker could successfully distribute malware to lure users into revealing confidential information (Harris et al., 2013; Masamila, 2014).

Mobile payments potentially give rise to confusion for consumers if problems arise as these services involve a number of companies across the financial services, communications sectors and third party intermediaries. It is not readily apparent to customers, what should be done if things go wrong, for example, if the phone is lost or stolen, or when customers need to correct wrongful transactions or suspect any fraud (Scribbins, 2013).

From the financial integrity perspective, mobile payments may be considered a good tool for reducing reliance on the use of anonymous cash, especially in countries that are predominantly cash-based as in Tanzania. However, according to Ally (2012) mobile payments may give rise to money laundering and financing of terrorism risks. On the other side, customer details may be abused by any member of the supply chain fraudulently to conduct transactions or other unintended purposes amounting to privacy violations (Harris et al., 2013).

All these security risks to mobile payment customers are most pronounced in the African context as the infancy of technologies and most nations have inadequate laws and institutions to confront serious cyber threats, monitor networks and remediate threats, of which are significant barriers to entry for low-income groups (Harris et al., 2013).

2.7   Strategies for addressing security risks on mobile payment customers

Mobile payments bring new opportunities and a number of risks to users. The customers are more exposed to risk because several parties are involved in performing the payment service. This multiparty transaction environment is conducive to fraudsters using both technological and sociological attacks. Therefore a careful planning that incorporates all the stakeholders is needed to ensure appropriate control and accountability mechanisms (OECD, 2012).

The identification of potential threats to mobile payment users is the key factor for security strategies. Mobile payment applications developed for mobile money services must be examined thoroughly to identify threat scenarios, such as spoofing, tampering, repudiation, and information disclosure. Protecting sensitive information stored on the mobile phone and strong authentication, is a necessary consideration (ISACA, 2011).

ISACA (2011) proposes the mitigation of mobile payment threats to customers is to deploy Trusted Service Manager (TSM) architecture. The TSM is collaborative across technical and business boundaries. Its functions would include such things as management of business rules and authentication, providing connectivity between MNOs and service providers, ensuring end-to-end security and end-to-end customer support.

Just as a chain is only as strong as its weakest link, specific attention needs to be put at each point of a mobile transaction; device and the user. The mobile payment service providers need to implement the appropriate privacy and security governance programs despite the lack of clear regulation. Users need to be educated to overcome the likelihood of risks on the mobile payments and mobile device manufacturers need to collaborate with the payment industry to ensure a secure environment for conducting mobile transactions (Gajda, 2011; Pegueros, 2012).

2.8 Importance of managing security risks to consumers on the mobile payments

The mobile payments are evolving rapidly in the developing world where they are attracting greater customer acceptance. However, security factors are remarked to influence the customers' decision by fearing financial, data and device losses, fraud, identity theft and others. This calls for the institutional and legal powers to protect consumers (Federal Reserve, 2013).

Thus, responsibilities for security in the mobile infrastructure span multiple participants, since risks faced by banks offering mobile payments are aligned with the risks that are perceived by customers and other stakeholders. So in order to achieve a secure chain of events each part of the network must seek to uphold the individual protection or else it would fall upon the false assumption that the other parts always would cover for the weak link (Federal Reserve, 2013).

Consumer security needs to be keenly addressed since it is crucial for the prosperity of mobile payment system as an alternative form of payment mechanism (Ally, 2012). Secure mobile payment acceptance supports consumer confidence and have the opportunity to reach a large proportion of the earth's population without the need for a large investment in technology (GSMA, 2014).

Despite the fact that it is very hard to create a completely secure mobile payment ecosystem for customers, the players should set security programs that ensure the cost of a successful attack is larger than the potential profit. However, it has been found that management of the mobile payment risks to consumers is higher institutionalized in developed than developing countries. This literature finding indicates the urgent need for the solutions to the potential security threats facing customers on the mobile payments in the developing world, particularly in Tanzania.

2.9 The models for securing customers on the mobile payments

The purpose of this section is to learn and conceptualize the liability of securing customers on the mobile payments, the strategies and considerations that should be made in the crafting the proposed framework to address security risks on customers in Tanzania. To check their synchronization with contemporary strategies in a proposed framework various perceptions of authors such as Trites et al. (2013), Wiedemann et al. (2010), Gadja (2011), Ally (2012), Pegueros (2012), Osikena (2012), GSMA (2014) and OECD guidelines have been analyzed.

After conceptualizing various ideas, two perspectives about the liability of securing customers on the mobile payments were realized. The first perspective includes the ideas that securing customers on the mobile payments is the liability of mobile payment providers, while the second one includes the perception that the customers are liable to secure themselves. These perspectives are discussed here under.

2.9.1 The model for securing customers by mobile payment service providers

This perspective is constructed on the arguments that mobile payments providers own and control IT and security infrastructure, they are competent on security technicalities, information systems and they dictate terms of agreements, thus they need to empower customer for the promotion of mobile payment services. Trites et al. (2013), Wiedemann et al. (2011), Gadja (2011), Pegueros (2011), OECD (2012) and GSMA (2014) argue to support this perspective.

Trites et al. (2013) argues that customers use mobile phones to make payments via funds accessed through MNOs, MPSPs, financial institutions or third party operators and suchpayments are made via accounts held at the MNOs or financial institutions of which customers have neither control of their IT infrastructure nor their security control.

21

Osikena (2012) and Trites et al. (2013) further argue that consumers on one side and the MNOs, MPSPs and financial institutions on the other side do not have the same information, understanding or bargaining power, so it is critical that consumers should be treated fairly in their dealings with financial institutions. Thus consumers' protection is crucial to promote their confidence.

Trites et al. (2013) also points out that the provision of mobile payment service is typically governed by an agreement between the consumer and the service provider and these agreements include both terms in the agreement and terms imposed by law. As in many standard forms of contracts, the terms of the agreement have the potential to favor the service provider at the expense of the consumer. The OECD (2010) recommends that to offset such asymmetry, consumers are to be treated fairly by the service providers.

Wiedemann et al. (2011) argue that MPSPs must meet security requirements; otherwise customers may ignore the mobile payment services. Likewise, Ally (2012) argues that securing customers in the mobile payment is a condition for acceptance of mobile payments into actual usage and value added for the user. This realizes that security is an essential condition for mobile payment prosperity.

Moreover, the GSMA (2014) and OECD (2012) substantiates the mobile payment brands security liability that they need to continue to promote the adoption and development of mobile payment by ensuring that risk management practices are extended through customers' empowerments about their rights and obligations in mobile payments. This argument is supported by Gadja (2011) that mobile payment brands have to enable customers to understand the underlying risk mobile payments.

22

The survey, conducted by the Federal Reserve in 2013 indicates that the security issue is the major challenge of mobile payments adoption and the Inter Media (2013) points out that insufficient understanding between the mobile payment users is the key barrier to the development of mobile payment services. To overcome the likelihood of customers falling victims on the mobile payments, Gajda, 2011 and Pegueros, 2012 propose customers' education as the important and necessary tool to offset technical risks inherent in the mobile payments.

2.9.2 The customers responsive model

Gadja, 2011 argues that consumers need to treat their mobile phone with the same zealous protection as they do their wallets. Examples of what the consumers are required to do include, the use of strong password to access the payment application on the phone, never to share confidential information, especially the PIN, to download mobile applications from trusted sources and report to the MNOs immediately after the phone is lost or stolen.

Trites et al. 2013 also points that customers have the liability to protect themselves as they are responsible to seek knowledge and understanding of their rights and responsibilities in the event of a fraudulent charge, loss or theft of a device, or any error. Similarly, a consumer who does not fully read or understand the disclosure statement would be less likely to be knowledgeable about the mobile payments.

An analysis of these perspectives indicates that it is worth for all the stakeholders in the mobile payment ecosystem to have the common obligation for customer security, while the customers have also an obligation of protecting themselves and their devices while adhering to mobile payments set standards. Thus, both perspectives hold water in securing customers as supported by Gadja (2011) and Trites et al. (2013).

The OECD (2008) policy guidance encourages participants in mobile commerce to ensure that consumers are informed about potential security and privacy challenges they may face in m-commerce. It further recommends measures to limit the risks, like encouraging the development of security precautions and built in security features, encouraging mobile operators to implement data security policies and measures to prevent unauthorized transactions and data breaches.

The OECD (2012) e-commerce guidelines call on businesses engaging in e-commerce to enable consumers to make an informed decision. These guidelines further insist that payment providers should put in place appropriate safeguards to protect the security of their systems, and should encourage the adoption of such measures by all entities having access to consumer data related to payments.

The OECD 2014 recommends that governments, payment providers, businesses, civil society and other stakeholders should work together to provide mechanisms that consumers can easily access to determine what their rights and protection are when making a purchase and the extent to which protection may vary, depending on factors such as the payment mechanism used. The commitment of all the parties involved in mobile payment is essential to achieve this goal.

Thus responsibilities for security in the mobile infrastructure span multiple participants, since risks faced by banks offering mobile payments are aligned with the risks that are perceived by customers and other stakeholders (Federal Reserve, 2013). So in order to achieve a secure chain of events each part of the network must seek to uphold the individual protection or else it would fall upon the false assumption that the other parts always would cover for the weak link.

2.10   Related works

This study has reviewed some studies relevant to its subject matter. The following are some of these important findings:-

2.10.1 The explosion of mobile money services in Tanzania

The 2013 - 2014 studies on the mobile money in Tanzania, use, barriers and opportunities and the state of mobile banking in Tanzania and security issues reveal the explosion of mobile payment services in Tanzania since 2007 to date. These studies portray the growth of mobile payment services, the emerged business models through partnerships of the service providers such as banks, MNOs and MPSPs (Inter Media, 2013) and that more people in Tanzania have subscribed to mobile money services than bank accounts (Masamila, 2014).

2.10.2 The mobile money ecosystem:

A 2013 study on the state of mobile banking in Tanzania and security issues apart from the growth of mobile payments in Tanzania discusses the mobile payment ecosystem in Tanzania, its key players, their symbiotic relationships and roles they play in the ecosystem.

2.10.3 Security issues pertaining to consumers in the mobile money ecosystem

A 2013 study on privacy and security concern associated with mobile money in Africa revealed that lack of proper attention to the basic security features on users' mobile phones make users vulnerable to numerous threats. Furthermore, it reveals that security is a bilateral role between both user and the service provider (Harris et al., 2013). In combating these security challenges, collaboration of the prayers is proposed as the solution to customer's vulnerabilities on the mobile payments (Masamila, 2014).

2.10.4 Mitigation strategies of the security risks to customers in the mobile payments

Several studies on the mobile payments, mobile payment security issues and customer protection in the mobile payments propose the mitigation strategies of the security risks to customers in the mobile payment arena such as customer education (Pegueros, 2012; Gadja 2011), effective laws, collaboration of the involving parties and strong authentication (Scribbins, 2013); and mobile malware protection and enhanced mobile payment infrastructure (European Payments, 2014).

2.10.5 Developing the framework

Developing this framework involved utilizing suitable research approaches, methods and theoretical foundation from the existing risk management guidelines, e.g. OECD guidelines and the Australian/New Zealand Standard for Risk Management (AS/NZS ISO 31000:2009) and the International standard for the mobile payment security (ISO 12812:2011) which provide customer protection mechanisms and a safe environment for mobile payment services.

a) OECD (Papers, No. 204:2012): Provides guidelines for consumer protection in respect to regulations, consumer issues and payment technical issues in the mobile payments.

b) OECD (Papers, No. 236:2014): Provides guidance on issues pertaining to terms and conditions, privacy, security, confirmation, children and dispute resolution and redress.

c) The Australian/New Zealand Standard for Risk Management(AS/NZS ISO 31000:2009): This provides the model for implementing the risk management process, namely risk identification, risk analysis, evaluation, treatment, monitoring and communication.

d) The International standard for the mobile payment security (ISO 12812:2011): Facilitates consumer protection mechanisms, including fair contract terms, transparency charges, and clarification of liability, complaint mechanisms and dispute resolution.

CHAPTER THREE: RESEARCH METHODOLOGY

3.1 Introduction

In this chapter, the methodology of the thesis is presented. This includes the research purpose, research approach, research strategy, sampling selection, data collection and data analysis. Lastly, reliability and validity issues are discussed to find the quality standard of the study.

3.2 Research Design

Research design serves as the architectural blueprint of research work, linking design, data collection, and analysis activities to the research questions and ensuring that the complete research agenda is addressed (Kothari, 2004). A research design provides validity, usefulness and feasibility of the study (Adam et al., 2008). Within this context, research design would result into exploratory, descriptive or explanatory. Exploratory research focuses on what is happening, trying to discover new ideas insights. Descriptive research focuses on observing and describing the characteristics of a particular individual or group under investigation. While on Explanatory research focuses on establishing relationships between variables (Kothari, 2004).

Considering the objective of proposing a framework that would address the security risks to customers on the mobile payment ecosystem in Tanzania, this study was designed to be both exploratory and descriptive. The research is exploratory as it seeks to find ways in which the customers can be better secured on the mobile payment services. This goal is accomplished by investigating measures being implemented as revealed in the literatureand integrating them into a better approach for customer security on the Tanzania mobile money business ecosystem. This research is also descriptive because the data collected and analyzed describe what mobile money stakeholders think fit to secure customers on the mobile payment ecosystem in Tanzania.

27

3.3   Research strategy

Research strategy is a general plan that helps researcher in answering the research questions in a systematic way. An effective research strategy contains the clear objectives, research questions, data collection resources and various constraints that affect the research in different ways. A research strategy helps the researcher to define why a researcher is employing a particular research strategy and specific data collection methods (Saunders et al., 2009).

The research strategies for a researcher are survey, case study and action researches. Survey research is good for deductive research approach and answers questions of "who, what, where, how much, how many". It also enables researchers to collect large amounts of data and analyze them for further inference to be drawn from it. Action research emphasizes on the context and purpose of research, cooperation between the researchers and practitioners as well as the necessity of the implications of the research. Case study research is an empirical inquiry into a phenomenon, set within its real world context, especially when the boundaries between phenomenon and context are not clearly defined (Saunders et al., 2009).

The research strategy chosen for this research work is a case study. This chosen strategy helps a researcher to examine, explore or describe a phenomenon exhaustively in its natural setting, using multiple data collection methods to gather information and to employ the chosen research design, as exploratory and descriptive in particular.

3.4   Research approach

Research approachesare plans and procedures for research that span the steps from broad assumptions to detailed methods of data collection, analysis, and interpretation. The generally recognized research approaches are quantitative and qualitative approaches (Kothari, 2004).

Quantitative research is an enquiry into an identified problem based on testing theories by examining the relationship among variables and normally using data collection techniques, such as questionnaire. These variables, in turn, can be measured, typically on instruments, so that numbered data can be analyzed by using statistical procedures. The goal of quantitative methods is to determine whether the predictive generalization holds water. Qualitative research, on the other hand is concerned with subjective assessment of attitudes, opinions and behavior of a phenomena from multiple perspectives (Kothari, 2004).

For better interpretation and presentation of findings, this research has employed both quantitative and qualitative research approaches. These approaches are employed whereby questionnaires were used to collate information from mobile money stakeholders on their perception about customer security on the mobile payments. This was further analyzed to draw inferences about their opinions on these linkages. This process was also employed in order to get a nuanced understanding of the findings presented as narrations of the interviewers.

3.5 Location of the Study.

The main focus of this study was Ilala district that also bears the status of "a Municipal Administrative Centre in Dar es Salaam region". Ilala is one of the three Municipalities in Dares Salaam Region, divided into 3 divisions, 26 wards and 102 streets (www.dsm.go.tz/).

3.6 Study Population

A population is the total of all individuals who have certain characteristics and are of interest to a researcher (Adam et al., 2008). The target population for this study was the mobile payment stakeholders in Ilala district, in the Dar Es Salaam region, Tanzania which includes customers (users), issuers (MNOs) agents (vendors), regulators (government), and MPSPs (all companies accepting mobile payments) in Tanzania.

3.7   Data Sources

Data sources typically fall into two primary and secondary categories. The primary data sources are observations, personal interview and mailing questionnaires. Observation involves the collection of information by the researcher's own observation, while personal interview, the researcher follows a defined format and seeks answers to a set of pre-conceived questions. In the questionnaire, questions are mailed to the respondents with a request to return them after completion (Saunders et al., 2008). Secondary data source, include books, government documents, internet and other documentations. This study was based on both data sources.

3.8   Sampling process

Kothari (2004) defines sampling as a process of selecting units from a population of interest so that by studying the sample fair generalization of results can be made to population from which it was chosen. Sampling gives the chance to the researcher to reduce the resources necessary to do the study, as it permits more intensive scrutiny and concentration on fewer cases.

Sampling selection can be either probability or non-probability. Probability sampling elements are selected randomly and the probability of none selected is non zero and usually equal in all cases. This sampling technique comprises simple random, systematic random, stratified random, cluster sampling and multi-stage sampling. However, non-probability samples do not allow the researcher to determine the probability. The non-probability sampling technique includes accessibility, purposive, quota and snowball sampling (Adam et al., 2008).

This study employed non-probability sampling technique to draw a sample size of 300 basing on purposive sampling technique. This technique was used so as to make sure that the desired mobile payment stakeholders were only included in this study, as well as overcoming time constraints and unnecessary expenses (Adam et al., 2008).

3.9   Data Collection

Data collection is a systematic approach to gathering information from a variety of sources to get a complete and accurate picture of an area of interest (Kothari, 2004). Data were collected from December 2014 to January 2015 by using a structured questionnaire. The prospective respondents from the mobile payment stakeholders in Tanzania which include customers, MNOs, agents, regulators, banks and MPSPs were approached and requested to participate in the study.

3.10   Research instrument

A structured questionnaire was used as the data collection instrument (N=300). The questionnaire was selected because it enabled the investigator to be consistent in asking questions and data yielded was easy to analyze. The questionnaire was divided into six parts. Part I comprised the respondents'demographic data, such as age, sex, marital status and educational status. Part II sought to determine the respondents' knowledge about the potential security risks to customers on the mobile payments. Part III was aimed at finding out the respondents' opinion on the roles of the stakeholders in securing customers, while Part IV sought to determine the respondents' perception on regulatory issues in promoting customer security. Part V aimed at finding out the respondents' opinion on the best ways to secure customers on the mobile payments and Part VI elicited the respondents' knowledge towards strategies to be incorporated in an approach for securing customers in the mobile payments in Tanzania.

3.11   Reliability and Validity

To achieve consistent and accurate data a researcher needs to use valid and reliable tools. Thus, validity and reliability are of vital priority in research design. From the questionnaire design point of view the tool should be valid and reliable. Validity refers to the degree to which the

31

instrument measures what it is supposed to be measuring. On the other hand, reliability relates to the precision and accuracy of the instrument. If used on a similar group of respondents in a similar context, the instrument should yield similar results (Adam et al., 2008).

Some strategies were put in place to ensure reliability and validity of this study. Firstly, preliminary questionnaires were administered to ensure that the answers that were been solicited were well understood as it is and for the appropriate data to be collected. Secondly, the necessary questions that were not well understood were reframed to ensure the respondents understand the questions as it is intended to be. This helps to avoid the case where respondents answered questions based on how they understood it, but rather how researchers designed the questions. Moreover, follow-up was made during the data collection to enable clarifications and to ensure appropriate information is exchanged so as to get the required information. The structured questionnaire was also very important because the stakeholders were many and it gave a uniform base for analyzing responses.

Moreover, when the questionnaires were returned, the researchers checked through all of them to ensure all the questions were answered. Those that were not complete were isolated from the others, since incomplete questionnaires could not make the data complete.

3.12   Data Analysis

Data analysis refers to the systemic computation of certain measures along with searching the patterns of relationships that exist between data groups. It also entails categorizing, ordering, manipulating and summarizing the data and describing them in meaningful terms that they answer the research questions (Kothari, 2004). Today there are various computer software packages such as STATA, SPSS, MINTAB and MS EXCELL that are used in the data analysis process (Adam et al., 2008).

This study employed the Statistical Package for the Social Sciences (SPSS) v16. 0 to capture the collected data and then used MS Excel for analyzing the collected data. The data entry in the SPSS first started with formatting the Data View and Data Variable panels. Each question on the questionnaire and their closed ended answers were all shortened into smaller sentences that could be easily understood when the result is produced. All questions were then entered in the variable data, which serves as the headings for the various responses inputted under them. This was followed by number coding the various closed ended answers to the questions.

The next stage was entering the questionnaires in the SPSS whereby all entries and questionnaires were cross checked and mistakes corrected to ensure accuracy. The results were produced from the SPSS and Excel in the form of percentage tables and graphs, respectively.

3.13   Ethical Considerations

Research ethics are defined as safeguarding privacy, rights and welfare of the people and communities that form the focus of the study (Adam et al., 2008). In this study, the basic ethical principles were observed; respondents were made aware of their rights, consent, confidentiality and privacy and anonymity was achieved by not putting names on the questionnaire.

Figure 3.1:   Summary of the research methodology for this study

Approach	Types and chosen				
Research design	Exploratory	Descriptive	Explanation		
Research strategy	Survey	Action	Case study		
Research approach	Qualitative		Quantitative		
Sampling techniques	Non probability (Purposive)		Probability		
Data collection instruments	Observation	Interview	Questionnaire		
Data source	Primary		Secondary		
Data analysis tools	ANOVA	MINTAB	MS EXCELL	SPSS	STATA

Summary of the research methodology compiled by the Research, 2015

CHAPTER FOUR: RESEARCH FINDINGS AND DISCUSSION

4.1   Introduction

This chapter presents the findings of the data collected by using questionnaires which were used as the instrument for data collection. The researcher planned to administer 300 questionnaires from 26 wards of the Ilala district, in the Dar Es Salaam city. However, only 288 questionnaires were completed, representing 96% of the total disbursed questionnaires. Data presented here cover demographic information, respondents' knowledge about mobile payments and the associated risks, regulation of mobile payments, liability of securing customers and strategies to secure customers in the mobile payments ecosystem in Tanzania.

4.2   Demographic information

In all, 67% of total respondents are male, while 43% are female. With regards to the age groups of respondents, 4% are between 10 - 20 years, 31% are between 21 - 30 years, 46% are between 31 - 40 years, while 16% are between 41 – 50 years, 3% are between 51 – 60 years and 1% is above 61 years. The majority of the respondents, 41%, have secondary education, followed by 29% respondents with the tertiary education. Both, respondents with the primary school and 1st degree education tally with 15% each, the respondents with the 2nd degree are 1% while none respondents with a PhD. All respondents are mainly subscribed to the MNOs and banks for mobile payment services whereby those subscribed to both MNOs and banks are 52%. Likewise, 100% of the respondents trust mobile payment services only if those security risks to customers were addressed as shown in Tables 4.1- 4.3 below.

Table 4.1 Respondents by sex

Sex	Frequency	Percent	Valid Percent	Cumulative Percent
Male	163	56.6	56.6	56.6
Female	125	43.4	43.4	100.0
Total	288	100.0	100.0	

Table 4.2 Respondents by age

Age group	Frequency	Percent	Valid Percent	Cumulative Percent
10-20	11	3.8	3.8	3.8
21-30	90	31.2	31.2	35.1
31-40	132	45.8	45.8	80.9
41-50	45	15.6	15.6	96.5
51-60	8	2.8	2.8	99.3
61+	2	.7	.7	100.0
Total	288	100.0	100.0	

Table 4.3 Education levels of the respondents

Education level	Frequency	Percent	Valid Percent	Cumulative Percent
Primary	42	14.6	14.6	14.6
Secondary	117	40.6	40.6	55.2
Tertiary	83	28.8	28.8	84.0
1st Degree	42	14.6	14.6	98.6
2nd Degree	4	1.4	1.4	100.0
Total	288	100.0	100.0	

4.3 The potential security risks to customers on the mobile payment in Tanzania.

The first objective of this study is to examine the security risks to customers on the mobile payment in Tanzania. To fulfill this, the study seeks to answer the following sub questions.

4.3.1 What are your mobile payment service providers?

This question aimed at assessing the respondents' general knowledge over their subscription for the mobile payment services. All 288 respondents responded into this question whereby 151 respondents equal to 52% access mobile payments through both banks and MNOs while 137 equal to 47% are only subscribed to MNOs as shown in Table 4.4 below.

Table 4.4   Respondents' subscription on the mobile payment services

M payment service providers	Frequency	Percent	Valid Percent	Cumulative Percent
Valid Bank and MNO	151	52.4	52.4	52.4
MNO	137	47.6	47.6	100.0
Total	288	100.0	100.0	

4.3.2 What security aspects mostly concerned you on mobile payments?

This question aimed at assessing the respondents' security awareness and concern over the mobile payments. The responses into this question indicate that mobile payment users are mostly concerned with security risks such as loosing or having phone stolen 34%, privacy violation 26%, interception of payment information 24% and malicious software 6%. However, 10% of all respondents are concerned with these security risks all together as shown in Table 4.5.

Table 4.5   Security concern of the respondents on the mobile payments

Security risks	Frequency	Percent	Valid Percent	Cumulative Percent
Misuse of personal information	75	26.0	26.0	26.0
Interception of payment information	69	24.0	24.0	50.0
Losing phone or having phone stolen	99	34.4	34.4	84.4
Malware or virus attacks	17	5.9	5.9	90.3
All of the above	28	9.7	9.7	100.0
Total	288	100.0	100.0	

36

4.3.3   If security aspects are addressed, would you still be interested in mobile payments?

This question aimed at assessing the respondents' interests over the mobile payments if security risks are appropriately managed. All 288 respondents trust mobile payment services only if those security risks were addressed as shown in Table 4.6.

Table 4.6 Respondents trusts if security issues on the mobile payments are addressed

Service trust	Frequency	Percent	Valid Percent	Cumulative Percent
Yes, very interested	288	100.0	100.0	100.0

4.3.4   What are your expectations of the mobile payment services?

This question aimed at assessing the respondents' expectations over the mobile payment services. All 288 respondents responded into this question whereby 51% expect secure and available mobile payment services, 19% expect reduced risks of carrying cash and increased financial accessibility, 18% expect privacy assurance and 12% expect low usage costs and assured mobile payment services. These data imply that mobile payment users need a secured, reliable and reputable mobile payment ecosystem. Figure 4.1 below show these responses.

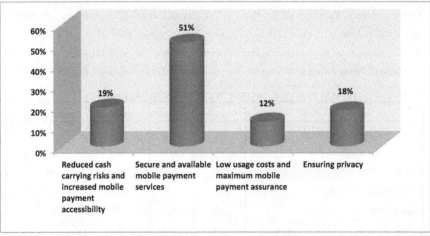

Figure 4.1:   Customers' expectations (Source: Field results 2015)

4.4 The stakeholders' obligations in securing customers in the mobile payments

The second objective of this study is to examine the obligations of stakeholders in the provision ofcustomers' security in the mobile payments value chain in Tanzania. To fulfil this objective the study seeks to answer the following sub questions:-

4.4.1 What roles should be done by the government to secure customers in the mobile payment services?

This question aimed at putting into right the government obligation in securing customers in the mobile payment services. All 288 respondents responded into this question and the responses show that, the government should provide laws, regulations and policies (49%), regulate mobile payment services (28%), educate customers (13%) and enforce laws in order to secure customers in the mobile payment. Figure 4.2 below shows these responses.

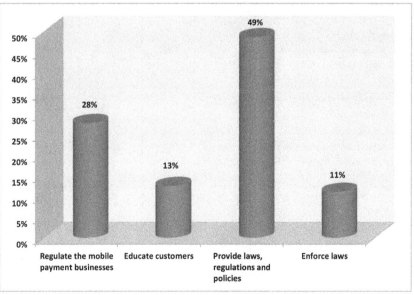

**Figure 4.2:   The government roles to secure customers on the mobile payments
(Source: Field results 2015)**

4.4.2   What can be done by the MNOs, MPSPs, financial institutions, the agents and merchants to secure their customers?

This question also aimed at putting into right the obligation of other stakeholders, including MNOs, MPSPs, financial institutions, the agents and merchantsin securing customers in the mobile payment services. All 288 respondents responded into this question and responses indicate that mobile payment stakeholders need toprovide sufficient e-money and cash at agent level (29%), ensure strong mobile payment security properties (26%), educate customers (21%), provide complaint handling and redress mechanisms (17%) and carefully handle customer information and comply with Know Your Customers (KYC) principles (8%). Table 4.7 below shows these responses.

Table 4.7   The roles of the mobile payment stakeholders in securing customers

Stakeholders obligations	Frequency	Percent	Valid Percent	Cumulative Percent
Ensure mobile payment security properties	74	25.7	25.7	25.7
Provide education and necessary information to customers	61	21.2	21.2	46.9
Provide complaint handling and redress mechanisms	49	17.0	17.0	63.9
Handle personal information carefully and comply with KYC	22	7.6	7.6	71.5
Ensure sufficient e-money and cash at agent level	82	28.5	28.5	100.0
Total	288	100.0	100.0	

4.5   Regulation of the mobile payment services in Tanzania

The third objective of this study is to examine the laws influencing the mobile money services in Tanzania. To fulfil this objective the study seeks to answer the following sub questions:-

4.5.1   In which ways laws can protect customers in the mobile payments?

All 288 respondents responded to this question and the results indicate that 37.9% proposed that laws can strengthen disincentives to mobile payment fraudsters, 25% proposed that laws canprovide remedies to customers over the mobile payment issues, 23% proposed that laws can provide complaints handling and redress mechanisms for the users of the mobile payments and 15% proposed that laws can control mobile payment risks to customers. Figure 4.3 below shows the percentages of these responses.

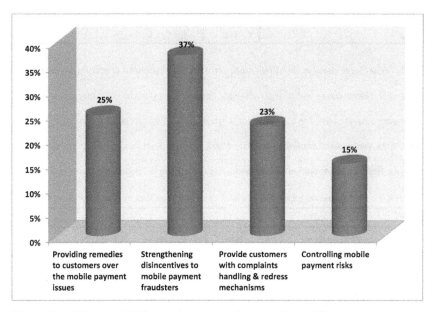

**Figure 4.3:   Ways in which laws can protect customers in the mobile payments
(Source: Field results 2015)**

4.5.2 Which of the following laws govern mobile payments in Tanzania?

All 288 respondents responded to this question and the results indicate that 43% no law, 20% not sure, 19% the banking and Financial Institution Act of 2006, 11% the Anti-Money laundering Act of 2006 and the Electronic and postal Communication Act of 2010 and 7% say that it is the Tanzania Communications Regulations Authority Act of 2003 as shown in Table 4.8 below.

Table 4.8   Response on the laws governing mobile payments in Tanzania

Laws on mobile payments	Frequency	Percent	Valid Percent	Cumulative Percent
The banking and Financial institution Act	56	19.4	19.4	19.4
The AML Act of 2006 and EPOCA 2010	31	10.8	10.8	30.2
The Tanzania Communications Regulatory Authority Act of 2003	20	6.9	6.9	37.2
Not sure	57	19.8	19.8	56.9
None of the above	124	43.1	43.1	100.0
Total	288	100.0	100.0	

4.5.3 What legal changes should be made for effective regulation of mobile payments?

Table 4.9 below shows some legal changes needed for effective regulation of the mobile payments, whereas 44% for enactment of a specific law, 29% for amendment of the existing laws, 15% prefer disincentives to fraudsters and 12% for improving law enforcement. These responses call for incorporation of customer security issues in the mobile payments in Tanzania.

Table 4.9   Reponsesto legal changes for effectiveregulations on mobile payments

Legal changes proposed	Frequency	Percent	Valid Percent	Cumulative Percent
Enacting a specific law to control	127	44.1	44.1	44.1
Amending the existing laws	84	29.2	29.2	73.3
Strengthening disincentives to mobile payment fraudsters	42	14.6	14.6	87.8
Improving law enforcement	35	12.2	12.2	100.0
Total	288	100.0	100.0	

4.6   Liability of securing customers on the mobile payments in Tanzania.

The fourth objective of this study is to examine the liability of securing customers on the mobile payments.To fulfil this objective the study seeks to answer the following sub questions:-

4.6.1   How can customers be better secured in the mobile payment?

The data collected which are presented in Table 4.10 and Figure 4.4 below show that customers in the mobile paymentscan be secured through responsiveness by all stakeholders (37%), the government (27%), customers (12%) and shared obligation (16%). Thus, shared responsiveness between customers and stakeholders is the best way of assuring customer security.

Table 4.10 Ways to secure customers in the mobile payments

Security obligations	Frequency	Percent	Valid Percent	Cumulative Percent
Responsiveness by all stakeholders	97	33.7	33.7	33.7
The government responsiveness	79	27.4	27.4	61.1
Customer responsiveness	53	18.4	18.4	79.5
Shared responsiveness between customers and all stakeholders	46	16.0	16.0	95.5
All of the above	13	4.5	4.5	100.0
Total	288	100.0	100.0	

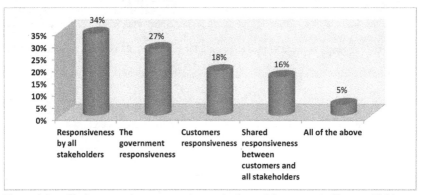

Figure 4.4:   Various ways to secure customers in the mobile payments (Source: Field results 2015)

4.7   Mechanisms for addressing security risks to customers on the mobile payments

The fifth objective of this study is to propose the mechanism for addressing the security risks to customers on the mobile payment ecosystem in Tanzania. The following questions were asked.

4.7.1   Which one explains the best mechanism of solving potential risks to customers

The collected data indicate that the respondents preferjoint efforts of stakeholders (41%), use of appropriate technology (287%), deployment of strong security properties and government intervention (10%) as the mechanisms insolving potential security risks to customersin the mobile payments. These observations are presented below in Table 4.11.

Table 4.11   Strategies for securing customers in the mobile payment ecosystem

Strategy options	Frequency	Percent	Valid Percent	Cumulative Percent
Joint efforts by all stakeholders	117	40.6	40.6	40.6
Deployment of strong security properties	64	22.2	22.2	62.8
Use of appropriate technology	78	27.1	27.1	89.9
Government interventions	29	10.1	10.1	100.0
Total	288	100.0	100.0	

4.7.2   Which strategies should be the core of the proposed framework

The results indicate that 56% suggest a risk management approach, 32% prefer research approach, 7% suggest trial and error method, and the remaining 5% propose reduction method. However, both risk management and research approaches seem to be more meaningful to this study. The risk management approach will determine the processes, techniques, tools, and team responsibilities for addressing security risks to customers on the mobile payments in Tanzania while investing in research should be a top priority in exploring fundamental challenges, identifying and test new solutions in securing customers.

43

CHAPTER FIVE: THE FRAMEWORK TO SECURE CUSTOMERS

5.1 Introduction

This chapter presents the proposed framework for addressing security risks to customers on the mobile payment in Tanzania. The details of the proposed framework, its core elements, implementation, governance and implication are hereby discussed in addressing the research topic.

5.2 The proposed framework

This research aims at proposing a framework that can be used to secure customers on the mobile payments in Tanzania. The proposed framework incorporates stakeholders' obligations to secure customers and constitutes collaboration of these stakeholders on the viewpoint of customer protection as a competitive strategy for the mobile payment market. This framework provides a common language for understanding of all key players in managing the mobile payment potential security threats to customers and it is a tool for aligning policy, business, and technological approaches in securing customers.

This proposed framework is an established business process which has incorporated measures proposed by various scholars, including Thomas et al (2005), Gadja (2011), Pegueros (2012), Scribbins (2013) and others. It has also adopted international industry standards and guidelines, e.g. OECD (2012) Report on Consumer Protection in Online and Mobile Payments, OECD (2014) Consumer Policy Guidance on Mobile and Online Payments; AS/NZS ISO 31000:2009 the Australian/New Zealand standards for risk management principles & guidelines, ISO 12812:2011, an International standard for the mobile payments and other guidelines. Moreover, other inputs obtained from field results were helpful in crafting this framework. Summary of the proposed framework is illustrated in figure 5.1.

The proposed framework for managing security risks to customers in the mobile payments

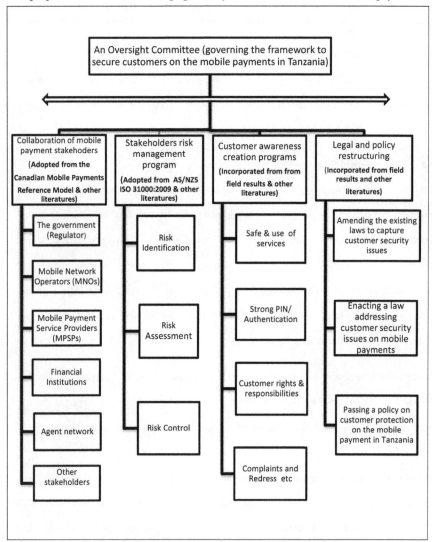

Figure 5.1:   The framework for managing security risks to customers in the
mobile payments(Source: The researcher, 2015)

5.3   The framework core elements

This framework is intended to provide the way forward in managing the potential security risks to customers in the mobile payments in Tanzania. Customer security has been recognized as a necessary component in maintaining the confidentiality, royalty, trust, reputation and promoting adaptability of the mobile payment system and financial inclusion.

Thus, based on the roles of the stakeholders, prevailing legal gaps in the regulation of mobile payments, issues of customer awareness and the need for a systemic and effective approach for managing security risks to customers on the mobile payment in Tanzania, this framework is formed by a set of four core elements. These core elements are basic program functions that form the foundation of for managing security risks to customers on the mobile payment in Tanzania. These include:-

☐ Collaboration of mobile payment stakeholders in managing security risks to customers in the mobile payments in Tanzania.

☐ Stakeholders risk management program on the security risks to customers in the mobile payments in Tanzania.

☐ Legal and policy reforms on mobile payment in Tanzania to accommodate issues pertaining to consumer protection, remedies to customers, mobile payment threats and security risks, dispute resolution and redress and others.

☐ Customer awareness creation programs on the mobile payment threats and security risksto consumers, customer protection, remedies to customers, appropriate dispute resolution and redress system available in the mobile payment system in Tanzania

5.3.1 Collaboration of the mobile payment stakeholders

Customer security is everyone's business in the mobile payment ecosystem. Cooperation between players in the mobile payment value chain drives customer retention, loyalty and responds to fundamental demand from customersas proposed by the OECD (2012). The cooperation of the mobile payment stakeholders was succeeded in Canada whereby the Canadian Mobile Payments Reference Model was developed to ensure a safe, secure and easy-to-use network for consumers as indicated by Trites et al. (2013).

However, the stakeholders' collaboration needs a careful planning and an integration of planning, customer security management programs and operational processes to ensure appropriate control and accountability mechanisms as pointed by Masamila (2014) and the field results. Therefore, stakeholders' cooperation should compel all mobile payment stakeholders accountable for managing risks to their customers.

5.3.2 Stakeholders risk management program

This framework has adopted the risk management approach consistent with the Australian /New Zealand standards for risk management (AS/NZS ISO 31000:2009) guidelines. The risk management is defined bythe AS/NZS ISO 31000:2009as the systematic application of management policies, procedures and practices to the tasks of identifying, assessing and controlling risks.It is an iterative process that, with each cycle, can contribute progressively to organizational improvement by providing management with a greater insight into risks and their impact. This risk management standard was adopted as the model to ensure clear, feasible and consistent risk management practices in managing security risks to customers on the mobile payment arena in Tanzania.

5.3.3 Legal and policy reforms

The field results and literatures reviewed for this study indicate the need for legal and policy reforms to accommodate mobile payments issues, so as to balance the interest of the customers and those of market players. Such reforms can be achieved through enacting a specific law, amending other laws pertinent to mobile payments and crafting a policy which accommodates mobile payment transactions, mobile payment security issues and customer protection as among the important things so as to make this framework implementable and successful in Tanzania.

Legal and policy reforms, together with stakeholders and feasible risk management programs should be considered as a package to enable this framework to manage effectively the security risks to customers in the mobile payment ecosystem in Tanzania. However, mobile payment legal and policy systems need to be dynamic as well as the whole framework since mobile payments technologies are evolving tremendously and the customer issues are volatile.

5.3.4 Customer awareness programs

Mobile payments users need to be educated to overcome the likelihood of falling victims according to the field results and literatures reviewed. The GSMA (2014) and OECD (2012), in particular, propose that risk management practices should be extended through customers' empowerments about their rights and obligations in mobile payments so as to promote its adoption and development.

Likewise, Gadja (2011) and Pegueros, (2012 are proposing effective customer capacity building program as anecessary tool to offset the higher technical risks inherent in mobile payment technologies to enable customers to understand the underlying risk of mobile payments. However, for this framework to succeed, customer education program should be made mandatory to all mobile payment stakeholders in Tanzania.

5.4 Implementation of the framework

This framework is expecting to address the potential security risks to customers in the mobile payment in Tanzania in accordance with the accredited risks management standards and guidelines like OECD Guidelines (OECD Digital Economy Papers, No. 204:2012 and OECD Digital Economy Papers, No. 236:2014); the Australian/New Zealand Standard for Risk Management (AS/NZS ISO 31000:2009) and the International standard for the mobile payment security (ISO 12812:2011) which provides customer protection mechanisms and a safe environment so that consumers can trust the mobile payment services. This framework will use the elements of aforementioned industry standards and guidelines as the model for securing customers in the mobile payments in Tanzania.

The proposed framework can be used by all mobile payment stakeholders as a key part of their systematic process for managing security risk to their customers. The framework is not proposed to replace existing processes; the mobile payment stakeholders can use their current process and overlay it into the framework to determine gaps in the current customer security risk approach and develop a roadmap to improvement.

The proposed framework is expected to complement existing business and customer security operations. It will serve as the foundation for a new customer security program or a mechanism for improving an existing program. It will provide a means of expressing customer security requirements to business partners and can help to identify gaps in an organization's customer security practices.

The following subsections illustrate how the mobile payment stakeholders can implement this framework to improve the existing customer security programs.

5.4.1 Reviewing customer security program

Implementation of this framework requires all mobile payment players to review their current customer security program and evaluate the probability of risk and estimate the impact so as to examine the extent to which they are achieving the security levels outcomes; Identify, Protect, Detect, Respond and Recover. These function levels provide a concise way of assessing how risks are managed and how the existing security standards, guidelines and practices are achieved.

Some players may find that they are already achieving the desired outcomes, while others may determine opportunities for improvement. Stakeholders should compare the current customer security program and the desired security program to determine gaps so as to move in a more informed and strengthened way to customer security practices where and when deemed fit.

5.4.2 Prioritize and scope

All mobile payment stakeholders should identifytheir business visions, missions, objectives and priorities in securing customers. This step is vital for developing an action plan to strengthen the existing and the desired customer security programs. Then, the stakeholders need to create a prioritized action plan and determine the resources necessary to address those gaps to achieve the target profile and make strategic and informed decisions regarding customer security programs.

5.4.3 Identifying potential security risks to customers

To build an effective risk management strategy, mobile payment stakeholders need to identify their customers' vulnerabilities in the operations of their deployment. The objective to identify and assess the risks to customers on the mobile payments should be to protect the customers from mobile payment risks, while also ensuring the service remained accessible and easy to use. That robust risk management strategy would be foundational to building trust with customers.

5.4.4 Assessing security risks to customers

In assessing the potential security risks to customers, the mobile payment stakeholders should consider the results of the ongoing monitoring relating to the services offered, technology solutions in use, services outsourced, application architecture, programming techniques and routines relevant to their own operations. Stakeholders should determine whether and to what extent changes may be necessary to the existing security measures and the time required to implement the required changes to protect and secure customers.

5.4.5 Creating a target profile

The mobile payment stakeholders should create a Security Target Profile that focuses on the risk assessment describing desired customer security outcomes. Stakeholders may also consider influences and requirements of external stakeholders such as sector entities, and business partners when creating a Target Profile.

5.4.6 Determining, analyzing, and prioritizing gaps

Stakeholders should compare the current profile and the target profile to determine gaps. Then, the stakeholders need to create a prioritized action plan and determine the resources necessary to address those gaps to achieve the outcomes in the target profile and make informed decisions about customer security programs.

5.4.7 Implementing action plan

The stakeholders should determine which actions to take in regards to the gaps, if any, identified in the previous step. Implementation of the action plan will ensure the communication strategies, monitoring for changes and concerns of existing or new stakeholders and the risk control decision will be communicated to all involving stakeholders. Hence a successful control will underpin, but not block, sustainable mobile payment commercial growth.

5.5 Guiding Principles for the framework

This framework would be guided by the following principles

a) Transparency:

The framework itself should be transparent to all stakeholders and the control strategies to address the potential security risks to customers on the mobile payments should be publicized.

b) International Standards:

Relevant national and international standards and guidelines should be adopted to address security risks to customers on the mobile payments. These standards should be reviewed to meet mobile payment customer security appetite.

c) Exercise of Statutory Authority

There should be strong laws compelling stakeholders to address security risks to customers', an implementation of this framework, together with an oversight committee to monitor the framework.

d) The cooperation between key players:

Cooperation between key players in the mobile payment business value chain is a significant approach of this framework. According to the Internet Security (2015), cooperation security approach fosters confidence and consensus, ensures collective responsibility and users' rights and enables global thinking. Thus cooperation should be made not an option but mandatory.

5.6 Framework governance

For the effective direction of the framework execution, an oversight committee should be established. The framework oversight committee should have a statutory basis to monitor the framework compliance of regulations, rules and procedures by all mobile payment stakeholders.

5.7   The framework implications

The proposed framework presented in this study gives rise to a variety of implications to customers, mobile payment stakeholders, the government and academicians.

The framework has implications to customers as they need to be informed of the mobile payments rules, procedures and their responsibility to secure themselves. Moreover, customers need to be guided with regard to the secure use of mobile payment services as it is likely that risks vary, even within a homogeneous market segment.

The management of this framework is centered on the government responsibility to provide a legal context that ensures that mobile payment schemes are subject to appropriate levels of customer security. Areas in which regulatory action may be needed include awareness and education among users of mobile payment schemes, the assignment of liabilities; the operation of complaints schemes, dispute resolution mechanisms and mobile payment security configurations.

For the mobile payment stakeholders, they need to consider their security policy and the risks their activity present to the mobile payment users. These mobile payment stakeholders need to carry on an ongoing basis, the assessment of the existing customer security schemes, clarify weaknesses, and identify alternative safeguards and legal obligations to secure their customers on the mobile payments industry.

For academics, the framework gives rise to a range of questions that are in need of research. Do customers have different risk-aversion profiles in a mobile payment context compared with electronic commerce and other conventional commerce? To what extent are mobile payment customers prepared to trade off convenience against payment risk? To what extent are various customer segments capable of understanding risk?

CHAPTER SIX: SUMMARY, CONCLUSION AND RECOMMENDATIONS

6.1 Introduction

The purpose of this research is to propose a framework that would address the security risks to customers on the mobile payment ecosystem in Tanzania. In fulfilling that objective, the study sought to put into light the potential security risks to customers; the roles of the mobile payments stakeholders in securing customers; the strengths of the laws; the liability for securing customers and the framework to address security risks to customers on the mobile payment. This chapter, therefore, presents the conclusions; recommendations, as well as directions for further studies.

6.2 Conclusion

Mobile payment is generally known as interactions among engaging parties regarding fund transfer and payments over a wireless network through mobile devices. The TCRA indicate that, the number of mobile phone subscribers in Tanzania is over 27 million among of which over 11 million are subscribed to mobile money services. This number exceeds the traditional banking services, of which are very dominant in urban areas. In this case mobile payments are the only available feasible means to provide mass market alternative to include rural area, which are characterized by low population density and poor infrastructure.

However, the growth of mobile payments give rise to a number of security threats to users, such as privacy violations, malware attacks, fraud, theft, deviations in the quality of services, financial and device losses, inadequate information and lack of proper complaints and redress mechanisms.Ignorance of users and lack of effective regulations are major causes.

A number of literatures about mobile payment have been discussing the security risks concern of the mobile payment users, none of them has formally addressed the problem in the developing countries particularly Tanzania. Moreover, several mobile payment frameworks had tried to address the computational load at engaging parties to overcome limitations of wireless environments, but they did not fully consider security issues for mobile payment users.

By synthesizing the potential security threats as identified in the literature review, this thesis has proposed a framework to help mobile payment stakeholders to address security risks to their customers. This framework is largely based on the knowledge created from empirical research; it has not yet been practically tested. The interest is to put it into practice to counter measure the potential security risks to customers in the mobile payment in Tanzania. For better management of the customer security programs, this framework should be reviewed time to time.

6.3   Recommendations
After doing this research, a researcher recommends the following:-

☐   Policy makers should consider strong regulation or standards and robust internal controls for mitigation of fraud risks to customers through legal restructuring to accommodate issues pertaining to mobile payments in Tanzania so as to bridge the prevailing gap.

☐   Policy makers should consider measures to standardize the national identification systems in Tanzania to counter ambiguities which expose customers in numerous vulnerabilities. Such policy initiative will improve ability to perform KYC and AML/CFT compliance.

☐   Service providers should work jointly in protecting their customers and must be compelled to create awareness programs to enable customers to understand about services available, terms and conditions and security issues of the mobile payments.

☐   All members of the mobile payment ecosystem should examine their mutual relationship and shared responsibilities in protecting their customers on the mobile payments and should adhere to the sectoral guidelines, standards, laws and regulations.

6.4   Areas for further studies

As for future work, the following studies arerecommended:-

a) The reasons behind mobile money users' perception that the mobile money is mainly for mobile money transfers.

b) The reasons behind mobile money users' perception on PIN sharing while aware that can make them vulnerable.

c) The empirical study in addressing the mobile money fraud.

d) The empirical study in addressing the mobile money interoperability problem.

REFERENCES

African Development Bank - ADB (2012). *Financial Inclusion and Integration through mobile payments transfer.* Enhancing Financial Integration through Sound Regulation of Cross-Border Mobile Payments: Opportunities and Challenges(Online). Available at: (www.afdb.org/FinancialInclusion/andIntegration/(Accessed 12th October 2014), p. 54.

Ally, A., (2012). *Legal challenges brought by the development of ICT in Tanzania.* An assessment of the growth of mobile banking services. The Open University of Tanzania (Online). Available at: (http://www.tita.or.tz/uploads/legal_ict.), p. 28.

Bank of Tanzania - BOT (2013). *Financial Stability Report, March 2013*(Online). Available at: (https://www.bot-tz.org), p. 52.

Bank of Tanzania - BOT (2014). *National Financial Inclusion Framework.* A Public - Private Stakeholders Initiatives, 2014 - 2016 (Online). Available at: (https://www.bot-tz.org), p. 52.

Clarker, R., (2008). *A Risk Assessment Framework for Mobile Payments.* 17 April,(Online). Available at: (www.rogerclarke.com/EC/MP-RAF), p. 30.

Consumer Protection Partnership – CPP (2013). *Report on the Partnership's work today and future priorities.* Priorities Report 2013-14(Online). Available at:(https://www.gov.uk/... /bis-13-1267-consumer-protection-partnership-future), p. 28.

Consumers International (2012). *A guide to developing consumer protection law.* Consumers International(Online). Available at: (http://www.consumersinternational.org), P. 32.

Daily Nation Friday Date: 16.05.2014 (Online). Available at: (www.ipsos.co.ke/), p. 37.

Di Castri, S., & Gidvan, L., (2014). *Enabling Mobile Money Policies in Tanzania.* A test and learn" approach to enabling market-led digital financial services (Online). Available at: (http://www.gsma.com/mobilefordevelopment/2014/Tanzania),p. 19.

Ernest & Young (2014). *Mobile Money.* An overview for global telecommunications operators(Online). Available at: (http://www.ey.com/telecommunications),p. 44.

European Payments Council (2012). *White Paper Mobile Payments.* Cours Saint-Michel 30A, B-1040 Brussels(Online). Available at: (www.europeanpaymentscouncil.eu/white-paper-mobile-payments), p. 95.

Federal Reserve System (2013). *Consumers and Mobile Financial Services*(Online). Available at: (www.federalreserves.gov/publications/default.htm), P. 79.

Gadja, B. (2011). *Managing the Risks and Security threats of mobile payment.* Lydian Journal (Online). Available at: (http://www.usa.visa.com/LydianJournal2011), p. 9.

Groupe Speciale Mobile Association – GSMA (2014). *The Mobile Economy.* Sub-Saharan Africa 2014 (Online). Available at: (www.gsma.com), p. 72.

57

Harris, A., Goodman., S.& Traynor,P.(2013). *Privacy and security concerns associated with mobile money applications in Africa.*Washington Journal of law, technology & arts, Volume 8, Issue 3, Mobile Money Symposium (Online). Available at: (http://www.digital.law.washington.edu), p. 20.

Information Systems Audit and Control Association - ISACA (2011). *Mobile Payments Risk, Security and Assurance Issues.* An ISACA Emerging Technology White Paper. November 2011. Rolling Meadow. IL 60008. USA. (Online) Available at:(www.isaca.org), p. 15.

Intermedia (2013). *Mobile Money in Tanzania.* Use, barriers and Opportunities. (Online) Available at: *(*www.intermedia.org/wp-content/... /FITS_Tanzania), p. 32.

International Organization for Standardization – ISO (2011). *The International standard for the mobile payment security (ISO 12812:2011).* International Forecourt Standard Forum.(Online) Available at:(www.iso.org/iso/catalogue_detail.htm?csnumber), p. 14

International Telecommunication Union - ITU (2013). *Mobile Money Revolution.* Financial Inclusion Enabler. ITU – Technology Watch Report, 2013. (Online) Available at: (http://www.itu.int/ITU-T/technowatch). p. 30.

Internet Society (2015). *Collaborative Security.* An approach to tackle Internet security issues.Available at: (http://www.internetsociety.org/internet), p. 6.

Israel, C., R., Alftredo M. S. & Meheut, V., (2009). *Ecosystem strategy Branchless banking in Kenya.* M-Pesa mobile money. Dial M for Money.(Online) Available at: (http://www.faculty.tuck.dartmouth.edu), p. 10.

Jamal, A., & Faustine, K. (2008). *Research Methods for Business and Social Studies.* Dar es Salaam: Mzumbe Book Project.

Jenkins, B. (2008). *Developing Mobile Money Ecosystems.* GSMA Mobile Money Summit, in Cairo, Egypt. (Online). Available at: (www.hks.harvard.edu/m-rcbg/... /jenkins_mobile_money_summer), p. 36.

Jenkins, C. (2013). *US Mobile Payment Landscape.*Two YearsLater(Online). Federal Reserve Bank of Boston (Online). Available at: (www.bostonfed.org/payment/2013/mobile-payments*)*, p. 28.

Karokola, G. R. (2012). *A Framework for Securing e-Government Services.* The Case of Tanzania (Online) Available at: (http://www.diva-portal.org), p. 128.

Komba, K. (2013). *Mobile Phone Financial Services Developments in Tanzania.* Mobile Payment Transactions-Security Audit And Assurance. ISACA Tanzania Chapter Workshop.(Online) Available at: (www.isaca.or.tz/), p. 21.

Kothari, C.R., 2004: *Research Methodology*: Methods and Techniques, 2ndEdition March 2013.

Lara, G., & Michael, J. (2012). *Managing the risk of Fraud in the Mobile Money*. GSMA Mobile Money for the Unbanked (MMU), p. 6.

Masamila, B. (2014). *State of Mobile Banking In Tanzania AndSecurity Issues*. International Journal of Network Security & Its Applications (IJNSA), Vol.6, No.4, July 2014. (Online) Available at: (http://airce.org/journal/nas/6414nsa05), p. 12.

Mike, G., Linda, L., & Scribbins, K. (2013). *Mobile Payments: Problem or Solution*. Implication for financial inclusion. (Online) Available at: (www.friendsprovidentfoundation.org/). P. 56.

Millicom (2014). *"Press Release", 10 September, 2014*. Stockholm, Sweden(Online) Available at: (www.millicom.com/media/1413005/tztigowekeza/), p. 2.

Organization for Economic Co-operation and Development - OECD (2014). *Consumer Policy Guidance on Mobile and Online Payments"*, OECD Digital Economy Papers, No. 236. OECD. (Online) Available at: (www.oecd-ilibrary.org/), p. 23.

Organization for Economic Co-operation and Development - OECD (2012). *Report on Consumer Protection in Online and Mobile Payments*. OECD Digital Economy Papers, No. 204. OECD(Online) Available at: (www.oecd-ilibrary.org/), p. 46.

Organization for Economic Co-operation and Development - OECD (2008). *Report Policy Guidance for Addressing Consumer Protection and Empowerment Issues in Mobile Commerce.*OECD Ministerial Meeting on the future of the Internet Economy. (Online) Available at:(www.oecd-ilibrary.org/...and.../oecd),p. 24.

Osikena, J. (2012). *The Financial Revolution in Africa: Mobile Payment Services in a New Global Age*. The Commonwealth. Foreign Policy Centre.(Online) Available at: (http://www.fpc.org.uk), p. 32.

Pegueros, V. (2012). *Security of Mobile Banking and Payments*. SANS Institute, InfoSec. Reading Room.(Online) Available at:(www.sans.org/securitymobilebanking-payments), p. 29.

Saunders, M. N., Saunders, M., Lewis, P., & Thornhill, A. (2011). *Research methods for business students, 5/e*: Pearson Education India.

Simpson,R. (2014). *Mobile Payments and Consumer Protection*. Consumer International Policy Briefing. (Online) Available at:(www.consumersinternational.org/mobilepayments), p. 12.

Smart Card Alliance (2011). *The mobile payments and NFC Landscape*. A US perspective. A Smart Card Alliance Payments Council White Paper, 191. (Online) Available at:(http://www.smartcardalliance.org), p

Stefan, J. (2010). *Managing the Risks of Mobile Money*. The Banking Agent Reform in Kenya". A Scenario Based Policy Analysis. CID Working Paper No. 45. April 2010. Harvard University. (Online) Available at:(http://www.hks.harvard.edu/), p. 91.

Tarafa za Kata na Mitaa za wilaya ya Ilala. (Online) Available at: (www.dsm.go.tz/).

The Australian/New Zealand Standard for Risk Management - AS/NZS ISO 31000 (2009). *Risk Management*. Principles and Guidelines. Standards Australia/Standards New Zealand. ISBN 0 7337 9289 8. (Online) Available at:(www.standards.co.nz/news/standards-information/risk-managment/), p. 10.

The Parliamentary Acts of Tanzania (2014). *POLiS* – Parliamentary Online Information System. (Online) Available at:(www.parliament.go.tz/index.php/documents/acts/)

Trites, S., Gibney, C. & Levesque, B. (2013). Mobile Payments and Consumer Protection in Canada. Financial Consumer Agenda of Canada. (Online) Available at:www.fcac.acfc.gc.ca/.../fcac_mobilepaymentsconsumerprotection), p. 65.

Uchena, C. E., Gerald, G.G., Ademu, J. & Tella, A. S. (2008). Medelling Usser Trust and Mobile Payment Adoption. A Conceptual Framework. Journal(Online) Available at: (www.ibimapublishing.com/journal/), P. 8.

United Nations Conference on Trade and Development - UNCTAD (2012). *Mobile Money for Business Development in East African Community (EAC)*. A Comparative Study of Existing Platforms and Regulations. (Online) Available at: (http://www.unctad.org/en/PublicationsLibrary/dtlstict2012d2_en.), p. 66.

United States Agency for International Development - USAID(2012). *Standards and Practices for Electronic and Mobile Payments*. Global Broadband and Innovations.(Online) Available at:(http://nethope.org/assets/uploads/ElecrtonicPaymretStandardsandReport), p. 118.

United States Agency for International Development - USAID(2013).*Tanzania Mobile Money Assessment and Case Study*. Examining cash payment streams and their electronic alternatives among USAID implementing partners.(Online) Available at:(http://www.solutionscenter.nethope.org), p 71.

Wiedmann, D., Linck, K., & Pousttchi, K. (2011). *Customer issues in Mobile Payment from the Customer viewpoint* (Online). Available at: (https://ideas.repec.org/p/pra/mprapa/2923.htm), p. 11.

Whitman, M. E., & Mattord, H., J. (2012). *Principles of Information Security*. Fourth Edition, 20 Channel Center, Boston, MA 02210. USA (Online) Available at: (www.cengagebrain.com/whitman38214)

APPENDICES   QUESTIONNAIRE

Statement of Confidentiality

My name is *Ireneus R. Mathias*, pursuing MSc in Information Technology & Management at Avinashilingam University/IFM. I am inviting you to participate in a study entitled "A framework for addressing the potential security risks to customers on the mobile payment ecosystem in Tanzania". This questionnaire aims at soliciting opinions to address the potential security customers on the mobile payments. The result will not be analyzed, shared or used in any unlawful manner and your confidentiality will be respected (**Tick the most option of your preference**).

PART I: Demographic information

1   Respondent Mobile Tel Number_____Date of Interview_____Time_____

2   Gender: Male [ ];   Female [ ];

3   Age: 15-20 [ ];   21-25 [ ];   26-45 [ ];   46-60 [ ];   61+ [ ]

4   Education: Primary[ ]; Secondary[ ]; Tertiary[ ]; 1st Degree[ ]; 2nd Degree[ ]; PhD[ ]; Other_

PART II: The potential security risks on customers in mobile payments in Tanzania

5   Your mobile payment service providersis
     [ ] A bank
     [ ] A bank and an MNO together
     [ ] An MNO
     [ ] Not to say
     [ ] Any other. Please explain _____

6   What security aspects mostly concerned you on mobile payments?
     [ ] Misusing my personal information or identity theft
     [ ] Liquidity risks or delayed transactions
     [ ] Losing my phone or having my phone stolen
     [ ] Malware or virus attack or lack of complaints handling system
     [ ] All of the above

7   If security aspects are addressed, would you still be interested in mobile payments?
     [ ]Yes. I will be very interested
     [ ] May be in the future
     [ ] I am not sure
     [ ] I am not interested any more
     [ ] No. I will not

8   What do you expect on the mobile payment services?
     [ ] Reduced risk of carrying cash and increased payment accessibility
     [ ] Secure services and availability of mobile payment services
     [ ] Low cost of usage and mobile payment enabling
     [ ] Ensure privacy
     [ ]Any other. Please explain_____

PART III: Roles of stakeholders in securing customers in the mobile payments in Tanzania

9   What roles should be played by government to secure customers in the mobile payments?
[ ] Regulate the mobile payment businesses
[ ] Protect customers
[ ] Provide laws, regulations and policies
[ ] Provide customer education
[ ] Any other. Please explain _____

10   What can be done by mobile payment stakeholdersto secure their customers?
[ ] Ensure confidentiality, integrity, availability, authentication and non-repudiation
[ ] Provide education and necessary information to customers
[ ] Provide complaints handling and redress mechanisms
[ ] Careful handling of personal information and KYC compliance
[ ] Ensure sufficient electronic money and hard cash at agent level

PART IV: Laws influencing the regulation of mobile payments in Tanzania

11   In which way laws can protect customers in the mobile payments?
[ ] Providing remedies to customers over the mobile payment issues
[ ] Strengthening disincentives to mobile payment fraudsters
[ ] Providing customers with complaints handling and redress mechanism
[ ] Controlling mobile payment risks
[ ] Any other. Please explain _____

12   Which of the following laws governs mobile payments in Tanzania?
[ ] The Banking and Financial Institutions Act of 2006;
[ ] The Anti-Money Laundering Act, & The Electronic and Postal Communications Act,
[ ] The Tanzania Communications Regulatory Authority Act of 2003.
[ ] Not sure
[ ] None of the above

13   What changes should be made for effective regulations of the mobile payments more?
[ ] Enacting a specific law to govern mobile payment issues
[ ] Amending the existing laws to control mobile payment risks
[ ] Improving law enforcement cooperation
[ ] Strengthen disincentives to mobile payment fraudsters
[ ] Any other. Please explain_____

PART V: Liability of securing customers in the mobile payments

14   How can customers be secured in the mobile payment?
[ ] Responsiveness of all stakeholders
[ ] The government responsiveness
[ ] Customer responsiveness
[ ] Shared responsiveness between customers and all stakeholders in the mobile payments
[ ] Any other. Please explain _____

PART V: Creating the framework for securing customers in the mobile payments

15   Which one of the following explains the best mechanism of solving potential risks to customers
[ ] Joint efforts by all stakeholders in prioritizing customer security in the mobile payments
[ ] Deployment of effective security properties
[ ] Use of appropriate technology for protecting customers
[ ] Government intervention, including monitoring, policing, laws and regulations
[ ] Any other. Please explain _____

16   Which strategies should be the core of the proposed framework
[ ] Risk management approach [identification, assessment, and controlling risks]
[ ] Research [employing existing ideas or adapting existing solutions to similar problems]
[ ] Trial and error [testing possible solutions until the right one is found]
[ ] Reduction: transforming the problem into another problem for which solutions exist
[ ] Any other strategy. Please explain _____

17   Your   suggestion   in   addressing   security   risks   to   customers   on   the   mobile payments_____
_____

The End!
Thank you very much for your valuable time and cooperation. Your responses are greatly appreciated.

YOUR KNOWLEDGE HAS VALUE

- We will publish your bachelor's and master's thesis, essays and papers

- Your own eBook and book - sold worldwide in all relevant shops

- Earn money with each sale

Upload your text at www.GRIN.com and publish for free